PRAYERSCRIPTS
Speaking God's Word Book Within

THE PRAYER OF JABEZ

ENLARGE MY BORDER

30 Days of Prayers For

STEPPING INTO GREATER

TERRITORY

CYRIL OPOKU

PREFACE

"Jabez called on the God of Israel, saying, 'Oh that you would bless me indeed, and enlarge my border! Let your hand be with me, and keep me from evil, that I may not cause pain!' God granted him that which he requested."
—1 Chronicles 4:10 WEB

The prayer of Jabez is more than a historical record—it is a prophetic cry for all who long to break out of limitation and step into God's greater purposes. Jabez was not defined by his painful beginning; instead, he lifted his voice to the God of covenant and asked boldly for enlargement. God heard him. God answered him. And that same God is still enlarging the lives of those who dare to ask.

This book was birthed from that same cry. I, too, have walked through seasons where my territory felt small, my resources limited, and my influence confined. Yet I discovered that when you call upon the Lord with faith, He opens doors no man can shut, He breaks the chains of restriction, and He ushers you into spaces you never imagined possible. These prayers are not theory—they are battle-tested cries forged in moments of desperation and answered by the faithfulness of God.

Enlarge My Border is a prophetic prayer guide designed to help you step into expansion—spiritually, relationally, and materially. Each day's Scripture and prayer will lead you to break barriers, silence the enemy's voice, and embrace the new dimensions God has already written into your destiny. As you pray, expect chains to fall, boundaries to shift, and heaven's enlargement to manifest in your life and family.

This is not just a prayer book—it is an invitation to transformation. May these words ignite your faith, fuel your intercession, and position you for the life of abundance and influence God has destined for you.

Expanding His Borders,
Cyril O. *(Illinois, August 2025)*

How to Use This Book

Enlarge My Border: Stepping Into Greater Territory is designed as a daily companion to guide you into a prophetic lifestyle of enlargement—spiritually, relationally, and materially. This is not just a devotional; it is a prayer journey meant to position you to walk in the fullness of God's promises. Here's how to make the most of it:

1. Dedicate a Daily Time:

Set aside a consistent time each day to engage with the prayer for that day. Treat this as sacred time with God, where distractions are minimized, and your heart is fully focused on communion with Him. Ten to twenty minutes daily is sufficient to meditate on the Scripture, pray, and receive revelation.

2. Begin with Scripture Reflection:

Each day begins with a carefully selected Scripture. Read it slowly, meditate on its meaning, and let the Holy Spirit illuminate how it applies to your life. Allow the Word to penetrate your spirit and prepare you to pray from a place of faith and expectancy.

3. Pray the Guided Prayer:

Use the prayer provided as a framework, allowing it to resonate with your own words and personal circumstances. Speak each declaration with authority and confidence, fully believing that God is enlarging your borders, breaking limitations, and establishing your territory. You may also pause to personalize the prayer for your specific family, career, or ministry needs.

- **Make It Personal**

  These prayers are written in the first person so you can make them your own. Speak them aloud, inserting the names of your family members, your workplace, your church, or your city where applicable. The more you personalize the prayer, the more you will sense its power shaping your reality.

- **Pray with Authority**

  These are not timid requests; they are bold decrees. Lift your voice as a covenant child of God, covered by the blood of Jesus and backed by heaven's authority. When you pray, do so with confidence that Christ has already won the victory on your behalf.

- **Leave Room for the Holy Spirit**

  These written prayers are a guide, not a limit. As you pray, pause to listen. The Holy Spirit may give you prophetic words, insights, or specific instructions. Follow His lead. Allow Him to expand the prayer, add declarations, or guide you into deeper intercession.

4. Journal Your Insights:

Keep a notebook or journal to record any thoughts, revelations, or confirmations you receive during prayer. Writing down what God speaks to you helps solidify understanding and creates a record of breakthrough and growth over time.

5. Repeat as Needed:

Some prayers or themes may need to be revisited multiple times. Spiritual enlargement is progressive; the more you engage with these prayers in faith, the deeper the expansion in your life and household. You can return to this book at any season to reinforce your territory and claim new dimensions of blessing.

6. Live in Expectancy:

Prayer is only one part of walking in enlargement—your actions, faith, and obedience amplify the power of these prayers. Move boldly into opportunities, embrace the doors God opens, and live with a confident expectation that your territory is increasing beyond what you can see or imagine.

By following this guide daily, you will cultivate a lifestyle of spiritual growth, divine increase, and kingdom impact. Let this book be your companion as you step into the new dimensions God has destined for you.

INTRODUCTION

"Jabez called on the God of Israel, saying, 'Oh that you would bless me indeed, and enlarge my border! Let your hand be with me, and keep me from evil, that I may not cause pain!' God granted him that which he requested."
—1 Chronicles 4:10 WEB

There comes a point in every believer's life when staying where you are is no longer an option. Something within you begins to stir, a holy dissatisfaction that whispers, *there is more.* More of God's presence, more of His power, more of His purpose at work in your life. The walls of limitation begin to feel too tight. The boundaries you've lived within—whether spiritual, relational, or material—start to press against your soul. It is at this moment that the Spirit of God invites you into the cry of Jabez: *"Oh that You would bless me indeed, and enlarge my territory!"*

Enlargement is not a selfish request. It is a divine yearning placed by God in the hearts of His children. It is heaven's reminder that you were not created to remain small, stuck, or stagnant. The God who spoke the universe into being is the same God who delights in stretching your borders, multiplying your influence, and causing your life to overflow with His goodness. To ask for enlargement is to align with the will of God, because He is the God of increase. He takes what is barren and makes it fruitful, He turns wilderness into fertile ground, and He transforms hidden lives into testimonies that shine before nations.

But enlargement does not come without resistance. The enemy's agenda is always to keep you hemmed in—boxed by fear, crushed by shame, limited by lack, or confined by invisible barriers. He knows that if you step into the territory God has prepared for you, your life will no longer just bless you—it will bless generations. This is why spiritual warfare often intensifies at the threshold of breakthrough. Every new dimension of enlargement must be contended for in prayer.

This book, *Enlarge My Border*, is a prophetic manual of prayers designed to help you break limitations and embrace the new dimensions God has destined for you. Through thirty days of Spirit-led intercession, rooted in the Word of God, you will cry out for expansion in your spiritual walk, in your relationships, and in your material provision. You will learn to confront the enemies of your enlargement and declare the promises of God with boldness.

Each week is a prophetic journey. In Week One, you will lift a cry for spiritual enlargement, asking God to break every ceiling and release breakthrough. In Week Two, you will step into courage and faith to occupy greater spaces of destiny. In Week Three, you will pray into fruitfulness and multiplication, calling forth abundance in every area of your life. And in Week Four, you will enter the overflow—living beyond limits, impacting generations, and carrying a legacy of enlargement.

Get ready to pray like never before. Get ready to shake off the restraints of the enemy. Get ready to stretch, to expand, to step into the wide-open spaces God has already written into your destiny. This is your time to enlarge your territory. The cry of Jabez is about to become your testimony.

WEEK 1:
THE CRY FOR ENLARGEMENT
(SPIRITUAL FOUNDATION)

Breakthrough Prayers for Enlargement

Theme: Asking God to break limits and release divine expansion.

Before God enlarges a person's territory, He first enlarges their heart and spirit. True expansion begins in the secret place, where desperation meets divine promise. The cry for enlargement is not a cry of greed, but of destiny—it is the prayer of a soul refusing to remain confined, limited, or bound by the works of the enemy. Like Jabez, who cried out for more, we too must lift our voices and ask God to shatter barriers and release divine expansion.

This week is about spiritual breakthrough. It is about standing at the threshold of something greater and crying to the Lord of increase to open new doors. It is the acknowledgment that without God's intervention, we remain hemmed in by circumstances, hindered by opposition, and limited in influence.

Prepare to pray boldly and prophetically. As you lift your cry for enlargement, chains will break, hidden ceilings will shatter, and your spirit will be positioned for the dimensions God has already destined for you.

DAY 1

BREAK MY LIMITATIONS

Jabez called on the God of Israel, saying, "Oh that you would bless me indeed, and enlarge my border! Let your hand be with me, and keep me from evil, that I may not cause pain!" God granted him that which he requested.
—1 Chronicles 4:10 WEB

O God of Abraham, Isaac, and Jacob, I lift my voice with holy boldness and decree enlargement over my life and family. You are the God who takes a small place and makes it wide; the God who turns barrenness into fruitfulness, and shame into glory. Today, I stand before Your throne and declare that every invisible wall erected against my progress is shattered by the power of Your mighty hand.

Father, I renounce every limitation that has held me bound—limitations of fear, ancestral curses, spiritual oppression, and demonic restrictions. I plead the Blood of Jesus over my household and command every chain of confinement to be broken. No longer shall my family walk in narrow places; You are leading us into wide and spacious territories ordained before the foundation of the world.

Lord, lay Your mighty hand upon me for victory and preservation. Shield me and my family from every arrow of evil. Silence the tongue of accusers, scatter the plots of wicked men, and frustrate the counsel of familiar spirits that seek to hold us back.

By Your Spirit, I step into new dimensions of influence, opportunity, and divine favor. I declare that my borders are enlarged spiritually, materially, and relationally. From this day forward, my story changes, and my family walks in the overflow of Your blessings.

In Jesus' name, Amen.

DAY 2

OUT OF DISTRESS

Out of my distress, I called on Yah. Yah answered me with freedom.
—Psalms 118:5 WEB

Mighty Deliverer, I lift up my cry in the day of trouble, for You are the God who hears and answers. From the narrow places of affliction, I call upon You, and You bring me into a land of liberty and expansion. Today, I rise in faith to declare that every distress laid upon me by the enemy is overturned. I renounce fear, oppression, and spiritual bondage, for You have answered me with freedom.

Lord, break the cords of limitation woven against my destiny. Destroy the snares that keep my family trapped in cycles of lack, sickness, or stagnation. By the authority of Your Word, I command the forces of darkness that afflict my household to be scattered. Let every prison gate swing open, and every door long shut against my progress be unlocked by Your divine hand.

Father, take me from the valley of distress into the mountain of enlargement. Remove every garment of heaviness and clothe me with songs of deliverance. Where the enemy has whispered defeat, let Your Spirit declare victory. Where men said, "It is impossible," let Your power make a way.

I prophesy that my life and my family shall not be confined. We step into wide spaces of joy, prosperity, and influence, to the glory of Your great name.

In Jesus' name, Amen.

DAY 3

SET IN A SPACIOUS PLACE

They came on me in the day of my calamity, but Yahweh
was my support. He brought me out also into a large place.
He delivered me, because he delighted in me... You have
enlarged my steps under me, so that my feet have not
slipped.
—Psalms 18:18–19, 36 WEB

Sovereign Lord, my Rock and my Fortress, I exalt You today.
Though the adversary rose against me in my day of calamity, You
became my shield. You lifted me from oppression and placed my
feet upon solid ground. I decree by faith that every storm sent to
confine my destiny is silenced by Your mighty hand.

Lord, I call forth enlargement into every area of my life. Deliver me
and my household from hidden traps and silent battles. Let the
arrows of the wicked be broken, and the pits they dug for me
become their own downfall. Because You delight in me, I will not
remain in tight corners. I step into the broad places of destiny,
prosperity, and fulfillment.

Father, steady my feet on the path of victory. Enlarge my steps so
that I do not stumble in weakness or fall into snares. Let every
generational curse designed to shrink my family line be swallowed
up in the Blood of Jesus. May my children and descendants know
only the freedom of enlargement and not the chains of
confinement.

I declare that the God who delights in me has brought me into a large place. I will flourish, I will multiply, and I will not be small. In Jesus' name, Amen.

DAY 4

ENLARGED AND PRESERVED

I will be glad and rejoice in your loving kindness, for you have seen my affliction. You have known my soul in adversities. You have not shut me up into the hand of the enemy. You have set my feet in a large place.
—Psalms 31:7–8 WEB

Faithful Father, the God of lovingkindness and covenant mercy, I rejoice in You. You have seen my pain and known the depths of my affliction. You have not handed me over to the will of my enemies but preserved me with Your unfailing love. Today, I rise to declare that my season of confinement is over.

Lord, every trap of the adversary designed to hold me captive is broken. Every force of darkness contending with my enlargement is consumed by Your fire. I decree over my family that no enemy will shut us in or box us into smallness. By the authority of Your Word, we escape the nets of oppression, and our souls are set free.

Father, place my feet in broad and secure places. Expand my influence, my capacity, and my vision. Let my family walk in wide and fruitful paths, where no adversary can overtake us. Scatter every evil alliance formed against our destiny, and let the hosts of heaven fight for our enlargement.

I declare that my days of affliction are turning into testimonies of increase. I will rejoice in Your kindness as You enlarge my borders and preserve my heritage. My household shall be a sign and wonder of Your abundant grace.

In Jesus' name, Amen.

DAY 5

STRETCH FORTH MY BORDERS

"Enlarge the place of your tent, and let them stretch out the curtains of your habitations; don't spare: lengthen your cords, and strengthen your stakes. For you will spread out on the right hand and on the left; your offspring will possess the nations, and settle in desolate cities."
—Isaiah 54:2–3 WEB

Great and Mighty God, You are the One who enlarges borders and commands increase. By Your Word, I rise in prophetic declaration: my tent is enlarging, my cords are lengthening, and my stakes are strengthening. I decree that every limitation assigned to restrict me and my family is shattered in the name of Jesus.

Lord, cause my life to expand beyond former boundaries. May my influence spread to the right and to the left. Let the desolate places of my life become fruitful, and let the barren cities of my destiny spring to life. I refuse to dwell in smallness; I embrace the call to enlargement ordained by Your Spirit.

Father, let my offspring rise in authority and possess the gates of nations. Let generational curses be uprooted, and generational blessings be established. Every tongue that rises against my expansion is condemned, and every hand stretched against my enlargement is broken.

I declare that this is the season of increase for me and my household. My borders are expanding, my inheritance is secured, and my impact shall reach to nations. To You, O Lord, be the glory forever.

In Jesus' name, Amen.

DAY 6

DELIVERED INTO SPACIOUS FREEDOM

> Yes surely he would have allured you out of distress, into a broad place, where there is no restriction. That which is set on your table would be full of fatness.
> —Job 36:16 WEB

Lord of Glory, my Deliverer and my Portion, I lift my voice in faith. You are the God who draws Your children out of distress into broad and unrestricted places. Today, I decree that every form of confinement around my destiny is broken by the power of Your Word.

Father, lure me out of the traps of the enemy. Break the chains of fear, poverty, and sickness. Let my household come out of narrow straits and step into wide, flourishing paths. Remove restrictions from my life and surround me with the abundance of Your provision. Let my table overflow with fatness, and my cup with blessing.

Every spiritual enemy that has vowed to reduce me, I command their power destroyed. Every adversary that stands at the gate of my enlargement, I rebuke by the authority of Christ. By the fire of the Holy Spirit, let the yokes of oppression be consumed, and let my freedom manifest.

I declare that I am stepping into a broad place of joy, health, and prosperity. My family will not be caged, and my destiny will not be confined. We walk in the fullness of enlargement ordained by Your mighty hand.

In Jesus' name, Amen.

DAY 7

FROM FIRE TO ENLARGEMENT

For you, God, have tested us. You have refined us, as silver
is refined. You brought us into prison. You laid a burden
on our backs. You allowed men to ride over our heads. We
went through fire and through water, but you brought us
to the place of abundance.
—Psalms 66:10–12 WEB

Almighty Refiner, the God who tests and purifies, I honor You.
Though we have passed through fire and water, You have preserved
us and brought us to abundance. Today, I stand in prophetic decree
that every affliction meant to destroy me is turning into a testimony
of enlargement.

Lord, I release the pain of past trials into Your hands. Where
burdens were heavy, You have lifted me. Where the enemy tried to
confine me in prisons of fear and lack, You have opened the gates
and ushered me into a land of plenty. I decree that no test shall limit
my destiny; every fire has refined me for greatness.

Father, destroy the plots of the wicked who ride over the heads of
Your people. Scatter the forces that contend with my enlargement.
Let the chains of affliction be broken, and let the river of increase
flow into my household.

I declare by faith that I and my family step out of trials into
testimonies, out of burdens into blessings, and out of confinement

into abundance. Our portion is enlargement, fruitfulness, and lasting increase to the glory of Your name.

In Jesus' name, Amen.

WEEK 2: WALKING INTO GREATER SPACES (DESTINY & POSSESSION)

Possessing New Spiritual and Physical Territories

Theme: Receiving strength, favor, and courage to occupy new dimensions.

Once the cry has been heard and God responds, the next call is to walk into the new spaces He has prepared. Enlargement requires courage. It demands that we leave behind the comfort of small places and step into the vastness of God's promise. Israel had to cross the Jordan to occupy Canaan; Joshua had to walk in strength and boldness to lead them. In the same way, you must rise to take possession of what God is releasing.

This week's prayers will focus on receiving strength, favor, and boldness to enter into greater dimensions. It is not enough for God to enlarge your borders—you must also possess the land. That means confronting spiritual resistance, silencing the voice of fear, and declaring ownership over the territory promised to you and your family.

Destiny is not inherited passively—it is seized actively by faith. As you pray through these Scriptures, the Lord will clothe you with courage, grant you wisdom, and release the favor needed to occupy new spaces.

DAY 8

ROOM FOR MY INHERITANCE

Isaac's servants dug in the valley, and found there a well of springing water. The herdsmen of Gerar argued with Isaac's herdsmen, saying, "The water is ours." He called the name of the well Esek, because they contended with him. They dug another well, and they argued over that, also. He called its name Sitnah. He left that place, and dug another well. They didn't argue over that one. He called it Rehoboth. He said, "For now Yahweh has made room for us, and we will be fruitful in the land."
— Genesis 26:19–22 WEB

Mighty God, the One who brings His people into a broad place, I lift my voice today with holy confidence. You are the God of Isaac, who makes room for His children when contention and opposition rise against them. I declare by faith that every enemy striving against my progress shall be silenced, and every power contending for my inheritance shall be scattered.

Father, as Isaac moved from strife to enlargement, so shall I and my household move from battles to breakthroughs. Where men have fought me, where envy and jealousy have risen, You are granting me Rehoboth. You are enlarging my portion and giving me room to expand without limit. The wells of my destiny shall no longer be blocked, and the living waters of favor shall flow unhindered in my life.

Lord of Hosts, I decree that every demonic embargo placed upon my family's advancement is shattered. Let ancient powers that contend with our opportunities dry up like wells in a desert. By Your hand, O Lord, release us into a place of rest, fruitfulness, and unending increase. No more shall my family be confined to Esek or Sitnah, but we shall dwell in the land of Rehoboth.

O God of enlargement, I receive open space, wide doors, and unhindered progress. My name is marked with favor, and my path shall shine brighter. We shall be fruitful in the land, and generations after me shall drink from the wells You have opened today.

In Jesus' name, Amen.

DAY 9

Every Place My Foot Treads

"I have given you every place that the sole of your foot will tread on, as I told Moses. From the wilderness, and this Lebanon, even to the great river, the river Euphrates, all the land of the Hittites, and to the great sea toward the going down of the sun, shall be your border."
— Joshua 1:3–4 WEB

Sovereign Lord, Possessor of heaven and earth, I come in agreement with Your Word that my territory is already given. The land is mine not by man's permission but by Your divine decree. I step forth today in faith and prophetic boldness, claiming every ground You have ordained for me and my family.

By the authority of Christ, I declare that every satanic giant sitting upon my inheritance must be unseated. I trample down fear, intimidation, and demonic opposition. Every boundary set by darkness is broken, and every ancient barrier collapses before the fire of God. Wherever the soles of my feet shall tread, I possess by the covenant of the Blood of Jesus.

Lord, enlarge my borders spiritually, financially, and relationally. Grant me courage like Joshua to face every battle, and grant me victory over the Hittites, Amalekites, and every power standing in resistance to my destiny. The wilderness is behind me; the promised land lies before me, and I shall not retreat until every promise You declared is mine.

Father, let my family walk in inherited blessings. May our children and children's children live in territories of peace, abundance, and dominion. No power of the enemy shall diminish our portion, for You have set the boundaries of our possession.

In Jesus' name, Amen.

DAY 10

GIVE ME THE MOUNTAIN

The children of Joseph spoke to Joshua, saying, "Why have you given me just one lot and one part for an inheritance, since we are a numerous people, because Yahweh has blessed us so far?" Joshua said to them, "If you are a numerous people, go up to the forest, and clear land for yourself there in the land of the Perizzites and of the Rephaim, since the hill country of Ephraim is too narrow for you." … Joshua spoke to the house of Joseph, Ephraim and Manasseh, saying, "You are a numerous people, and have great power. You shall not have one lot only; but the hill country shall be yours."
— Joshua 17:14–18 WEB

Lord God Almighty, the Giver of inheritance, I rise in bold prayer like the children of Joseph, declaring that my portion cannot be small. You have made me great through the power of the Cross, and I refuse to be confined to narrow places.

Today I speak enlargement into my life, my family, and my destiny. I declare that every forested place of limitation is cleared. Every stronghold of the Perizzites and Rephaim opposing my progress is uprooted by the fire of God. Where the enemy seeks to reduce me, You, O Lord, are multiplying me. Where the adversary tries to bind me in scarcity, You are granting me the hill country of abundance.

Father, I decree that no curse, no generational bondage, and no territorial spirit shall hinder my advancement. My feet are set upon new territories, and my hands are strengthened for war. The spirit of power rests upon me, granting me the capacity to expand, to build, to conquer, and to establish.

Lord, enlarge the boundaries of my influence. Let my family walk in greatness and my children inherit spacious places. We will not be hemmed in by darkness but will expand on every side. Our name shall be called blessed, and our portion shall never be diminished.

In Jesus' name, Amen.

DAY 11

ENLARGED BY OBEDIENCE

If Yahweh your God enlarges your border, as he has sworn
to your fathers, and gives you all the land which he
promised to give to your fathers; if you keep all this
commandment to do it, which I command you today, to
love Yahweh your God, and to walk ever in his ways; then
you shall add three more cities for yourselves, in addition
to these three.
— Deuteronomy 19:8–9 WEB

O Faithful God, Covenant Keeper, You are the One who enlarges
borders by promise and oath. You swore to Abraham, Isaac, and
Jacob that their seed would inherit the land, and I am a seed of that
covenant through Christ Jesus. Therefore, I stand to claim
enlargement by obedience to Your Word.

Lord, I bind every spirit of rebellion, compromise, and
disobedience that would seek to reduce my borders. By Your grace,
I walk in love, I walk in truth, and I walk in holiness. No enemy
shall accuse me before the throne, for the blood of Jesus speaks
better things on my behalf. As I walk in obedience, let every closed
gate swing wide open.

Father, enlarge the territory of my family. Multiply our inheritance
in spiritual authority, in possessions, and in generational blessings.
As You add cities, lands, and nations to Your faithful ones, so let
expansion be our portion. Let every land where our feet tread
become a land of dominion.

I decree that disobedience will not shrink us, and sin will not rob us. We are marked by obedience, and therefore we are marked for enlargement. Lord, stretch forth Your hand and bring us into wide, fruitful places prepared before time.

In Jesus' name, Amen.

DAY 12

ABUNDANCE WITHOUT MEASURE

Yahweh will make you abundantly prosperous in the fruit
of your body, in the fruit of your livestock, and in the fruit
of your ground, in the land which Yahweh swore to your
fathers to give you.
— Deuteronomy 28:11 WEB

Lord of increase, the God of more than enough, I come before You declaring that abundance is my covenant right. By the power of Your promise, I decree prosperity over my household. My body, my livestock, my land, and every work of my hand shall overflow with increase.

Father, I cancel every satanic decree of poverty, barrenness, and emptiness against my family. No curse shall swallow our harvest, no devourer shall consume our fruit, and no enemy shall diminish the prosperity You have ordained. From this day, we enter into a season of divine overflow.

Let the fruit of my body be blessed—my children shall rise as mighty arrows in Your hand. Let the work of my hands prosper— businesses, careers, and ministries shall flourish. Let the fruit of the ground yield increase—every seed I sow in faith shall multiply a hundredfold.

Lord, let my household be known as a family of abundance. May we lend and never borrow, give and never lack, sow and always reap. Enlarge us until our cup runs over and our barns overflow with plenty.

In Jesus' name, Amen.

DAY 13

YOUR CHILDREN SHALL RETURN

"For as for your waste and your desolate places, and your land that has been destroyed, surely now that it is too small for the inhabitants, and those who swallowed you up will be far away. The children of your bereavement will say again in your ears, 'The place is too small for me. Give me a place to dwell in.'"
— Isaiah 49:19–20 WEB

Redeemer of Israel, Restorer of ruins, I stand on this prophetic Word and declare life into every desolate place in my destiny. What the enemy swallowed, what was destroyed, what lay barren and wasted, You are reviving. The land shall no longer be desolate; it shall be filled with abundance and overflowing with sons and daughters.

Lord, every power that devoured my blessings is far removed. Every destroyer of my family's fruitfulness is banished. I decree restoration of wasted years, recovery of stolen inheritance, and multiplication of what the enemy thought was lost.

Father, enlarge my dwelling place, for the children of promise are coming home. My spiritual sons and daughters, my biological children, my destiny helpers—they are returning, and they shall say, "This place is too small." Increase me, O Lord, until I overflow with those You have destined to be part of my assignment.

God of restoration, I will not mourn in desolation but rejoice in multiplication. My land shall be fruitful, my house filled, and my legacy enlarged. What was once empty shall now be overflowing with life.

In Jesus' name, Amen.

DAY 14

DELIVERED INTO A BROAD PLACE

He also brought me out into a large place. He delivered
me, because he delighted in me.
— 2 Samuel 22:20 WEB

O Lord my Deliverer, You are the God who delights in Your children and brings them out into broad places. I lift my voice in gratitude and warfare, declaring that my days of confinement are over.

By Your mighty hand, I am rescued from narrowness, from oppression, and from the snares of the wicked one. No longer shall I dwell in restricted places. No longer shall my family be hemmed in by demonic limitations. The chains are broken, and the walls of captivity fall down flat before me.

Father, deliver me from every enemy that surrounds my destiny. Uproot every satanic structure built to restrict my progress. Shatter every invisible cage where the enemy has tried to confine my potential. Because You delight in me, You have decreed enlargement over my life.

Lord of Glory, I step into broad spaces—spaces of peace, prosperity, and divine expansion. My life will not be small; my future will not be restricted. Because You have delivered me, my household shall flourish in liberty, in influence, and in destiny fulfillment.

In Jesus' name, Amen.

Week 3: Fruitfulness & Increase (Material & Relational Expansion)

Fruitfulness And Multiplication in Life and Relationships

Theme: Multiplication, prosperity, and flourishing under God's blessing.

Expansion is incomplete without fruitfulness. God's enlargement always comes with multiplication, prosperity, and flourishing in every area of life. The barren woman sings for joy, the desolate places are inhabited again, and the righteous flourish like palm trees planted by streams of living water. Enlargement means God not only gives more space, but also fills that space with abundance.

This week, the focus is on fruitfulness in relationships, finances, and influence. The enemy's agenda is always to bring barrenness, waste, or stagnation, but God reverses these cycles and makes His people abound. Where there has been lack, He commands increase. Where there has been emptiness, He releases fullness.

As you lift prayers of fruitfulness, expect God to cause multiplication in your life. Expect divine opportunities, supernatural provision, and flourishing relationships that will bear kingdom impact. You are stepping into a season where "little" is transformed into "much" and where every seed yields an abundant harvest.

DAY 15

MULTIPLIED BEYOND MEASURE

He increased his people greatly, and made them stronger
than their adversaries.
—Psalms 105:24 WEB

O Lord of hosts, the God who multiplies His people and causes
them to prevail, I lift my voice in gratitude and warfare today. You
are the One who turns the few into many and the weak into mighty,
for nothing can resist Your hand of increase. Just as You multiplied
Israel and caused them to grow until their enemies were
overwhelmed, I declare that Your power is at work in my life and
my family.

Father, break every limitation set against my fruitfulness. Uproot
every curse of smallness, delay, and stagnation. I decree by the
authority of Christ's blood that my household will not diminish but
increase. Where the enemy has sought to confine, frustrate, or
oppress, let Your mighty hand expand us in numbers, in influence,
and in wealth.

Lord, cause us to grow in strength until no adversary can stand
before us. Let those who plot our downfall stumble and fall as You
lift us higher. Make us stronger than every principality assigned
against our progress, and let the sound of rejoicing never cease
from our tents.

I proclaim enlargement, multiplication, and divine flourishing. Our
generations shall rise in greater numbers, greater strength, and

greater testimony. Thank You for being the God who multiplies without measure.

In Jesus' name, Amen.

DAY 16

PLANTED FOR FLOURISHING

The righteous shall flourish like the palm tree. He will grow like a cedar in Lebanon. They are planted in Yahweh's house. They will flourish in our God's courts. They will still produce fruit in old age. They will be full of sap and green.
—Psalms 92:12–14 WEB

Majestic King, You are the One who plants the righteous in fertile ground, and You have destined me and my family to flourish like palm trees and stand like the cedars of Lebanon. I thank You that in Your courts there is life, strength, and unending fruitfulness.

Lord, uproot every assignment of barrenness, dryness, and decay. Where the enemy has sown weeds of destruction, let Your fire consume them. I declare that my roots run deep in You, and no storm of wickedness can topple my growth. Like the palm tree, I bend but never break, I endure and yet increase.

Father, let fresh oil and sap of Your Spirit flow in me daily. Even in advanced years, let fruitfulness remain my portion. My children and children's children shall not wither, but shall carry testimonies of strength, wealth, and spiritual authority. Let our legacy stand tall like Lebanon's cedar, unshaken and evergreen.

Today I declare flourishing in every area—spiritually, financially, relationally, and generationally. Our destiny shall not be cut short.

The wicked will not see our downfall, but they shall witness our rising glory in Your courts.

In Jesus' name, Amen.

DAY 17

RESTORED AND INCREASED

I will multiply on you man and animal. They will increase
and be fruitful. I will cause you to be inhabited as you were
before, and will do better to you than at your beginnings.
Then you will know that I am Yahweh.
—Ezekiel 36:11 WEB

God of restoration, the One who takes what was broken and makes
it better than before, I lift up my voice to declare Your promises over
my household. You are the Lord who restores cities and families,
multiplying man and beast, blessing generations, and causing
habitation to be better than beginnings.

Father, where the enemy has wasted years, let restoration flow.
Where he has diminished strength, stolen opportunities, and
suppressed growth, let divine compensation manifest. Multiply our
resources, multiply our offspring, multiply our influence until there
is undeniable fruitfulness in every corner of our lives.

Lord, let every desolate area of my family's destiny be rebuilt.
Where barrenness and emptiness once ruled, let abundance and
habitation arise. Make our latter days greater than our former, for
You are Yahweh who does exceedingly beyond the start.

I declare prophetically that our destiny is being restored,
multiplied, and lifted higher. No longer shall we dwell in lack or
oppression. Our story shall be one of restoration and greater glory.

In Jesus' name, Amen.

DAY 18

DOORS OF TREASURES OPENED

"I will go before you and make the rough places smooth. I will break the doors of bronze in pieces and cut apart the bars of iron. I will give you the treasures of darkness, and hidden riches of secret places, that you may know that it is I, Yahweh, who calls you by your name, even the God of Israel."
—Isaiah 45:2–3 WEB

Mighty Breaker, God of Israel, You are the One who goes before me, leveling every obstacle and shattering every gate of bronze. I exalt You as the God who calls me by name and delivers hidden treasures into my hands.

Father, break every spiritual prison holding back my destiny. Cut apart the iron bars erected by witchcraft, oppression, and ancestral limitations. Every wall the enemy has erected against my enlargement—collapse it now by the authority of Your word.

Lord, open up the hidden riches meant for my family. Bring out treasures buried in secret places and release wealth from unlikely sources. Where the enemy has covered our blessings in darkness, shine Your light and expose what belongs to us.

Today I decree enlargement into realms of wealth, resources, and influence. My family shall not live in lack but in abundance. You are my God, and You will demonstrate Your calling upon my life through visible prosperity and dominion. In Jesus' name, Amen.

DAY 19

Strengthened for Enlargement

So Jotham became mighty, because he ordered his ways
before Yahweh his God.
—2 Chronicles 27:6 WEB

Faithful God, You are the One who makes men mighty when they
walk uprightly before You. Just as Jotham was established and
became strong through obedience, I align my ways to You today.

Lord, destroy every enemy that wars against my alignment with
Your Word. Break the grip of compromise, delay, and distraction.
Every spirit of sabotage that seeks to weaken my household, I
command it to scatter in the name of Jesus.

Father, clothe me and my family with divine strength. Cause our
obedience to usher us into enlargement. Where the enemy has
sought to limit our progress, let might and dominion overthrow
their plots. May we rise above mediocrity and stand established in
authority.

I declare that my household will walk in holiness, integrity, and
divine order. We shall be mighty in the land, unshakable before our
adversaries. Our enlargement is secured, our strength is multiplied,
and our steps are ordered before You.

In Jesus' name, Amen.

DAY 20

FAITHFUL OVER FEW

His lord said to him, 'Well done, good and faithful servant.
You have been faithful over a few things, I will set you over
many things. Enter into the joy of your lord.'
—Matthew 25:21 WEB

Righteous Judge, You are the Master who rewards faithfulness with increase. I thank You that faithfulness in little qualifies me for much, and that You have called me into greater stewardship.

Lord, destroy every spirit of waste, laziness, and mismanagement in my life. Cancel the schemes of the enemy that seek to rob me of destiny through carelessness or distraction. Align my heart with diligence, wisdom, and excellence, that I may be counted faithful before You.

Father, enlarge my territory as I prove trustworthy. Let greater opportunities, resources, and responsibilities be released into my hands. May my family rise into positions of influence, handling much with faithfulness and multiplying what You entrust to us.

I declare prophetically that my season of smallness is over. The Master has spoken enlargement, and we shall enter into His joy. Our faithfulness will not be overlooked; it will be rewarded with dominion and expansion.

In Jesus' name, Amen.

DAY 21

LAUNCHED INTO OVERFLOW

When he had finished speaking, he said to Simon, "Put out into the deep, and let down your nets for a catch." Simon answered him, "Master, we worked all night and took nothing; but at your word I will let down the net." When they had done this, they caught a great multitude of fish, and their net was breaking.
—Luke 5:4–6 WEB

Lord of the Harvest, You are the One whose Word brings increase beyond human effort. At Your command, empty nets overflow, and barren seasons turn into abundance.

Father, I renounce every spirit of fruitless labor. Break the power of toiling without reward in my life and family. Where the enemy has wasted our nights with futility, let Your voice usher in a morning of breakthrough.

At Your Word, Lord, I launch into the deep. I refuse to be confined to shallow waters of mediocrity. Command the resources of the earth, the fish of the sea, and the wealth of nations to be gathered into my hands. Let every hidden harvest locate me now.

I decree and declare: our nets will overflow, our boats will be filled, and our testimony will be undeniable. Enlargement has come by the command of the Master, and no adversary can stop it.

In Jesus' name, Amen.

WEEK 4: BEYOND LIMITS (OVERFLOW & GLOBAL REACH)

Walking In Overflow, Legacy, and Generational Impact

Theme: Living in overflow, divine abundance, and generational enlargement.

T he final stage of enlargement is not just personal expansion—it is overflow that touches generations and nations. God's ultimate plan for His children is not survival or even sufficiency, but abundance that becomes a testimony to the world. When He enlarges your territory beyond limits, your life becomes a channel of blessing to many.

This week centers on overflow, legacy, and generational impact. It is about breaking every ceiling and refusing to live within the confines of small expectations. It is about rising into the "exceedingly, abundantly above all" life that God has promised. Enlargement is not complete until it extends beyond you, affecting your children, your community, and even nations.

As you pray through these Scriptures, expect God to position you for lasting impact. You are called to walk in overflow, to leave behind a godly heritage, and to carry influence that multiplies beyond borders. This is the week where you step into the fullness of enlargement—living beyond limits.

DAY 22

WISDOM WITHOUT MEASURE

"God gave Solomon abundant wisdom, understanding,
and very great understanding, even as the sand that is on
the seashore."
—1 Kings 4:29 WEB

O Lord of all wisdom and might, I lift my voice to You who holds
the treasures of knowledge and understanding. You are the Ancient
of Days, the One who enlarges the heart of Your servants and causes
their minds to overflow with divine insight. Father, as You gave
Solomon wisdom like the sand of the seashore, grant unto me and
my household a dimension of wisdom that cannot be confined or
resisted.

Every power of limitation assigned to cripple my vision and the
destiny of my family, I rise against you in the name of the Lord! I
decree that the wisdom of God enlarges my capacity and establishes
us in territories we could never enter by human effort. By the Spirit
of revelation, I receive divine strategies to break barriers, disarm
adversaries, and silence the tongues of the wicked.

I declare that ignorance, confusion, and demonic manipulation will
not rule my household. Our steps are ordered by heavenly insight,
and our influence is multiplied in every sphere. The Lord is
expanding our borders through the wealth of wisdom, so that
nations and generations will be impacted.

Father, thank You for stretching my capacity beyond limits. Thank You for making me a carrier of wisdom that shakes kingdoms and confounds the enemy. As You enlarged Solomon, enlarge me also, until my life becomes a testimony of Your glory.

In Jesus' name, Amen.

DAY 23

DOUBLE PORTION OF GLORY

"Instead of your shame you shall have double; and instead of dishonor they shall rejoice in their portion: therefore in their land they shall possess double; everlasting joy shall be to them."
—Isaiah 61:7 WEB

Mighty Redeemer, I exalt You who takes away shame and clothes Your children with everlasting joy. You are the God who reverses dishonor and crowns with glory. Today I declare over myself and my family: every garment of shame, reproach, and delay is consumed by Your fire, and in its place, You clothe us with the robe of double honor.

Every spirit of shame assigned to limit my destiny, I command you to be broken! Every ancestral reproach designed to confine my household, I cancel your hold by the blood of Jesus. I declare that we will not be mocked, we will not be diminished, and we will not be confined to small places. Instead, we rise into double portion inheritance—double favor, double influence, double possession of our promised land.

Father, cause the years of dishonor to be swallowed in sudden joy. Let the oil of gladness flow upon me and my children, turning every sorrow into dancing. Let divine enlargement break forth in our family line, making us a testimony of restoration and increase.

Thank You, Lord, for releasing double for all our troubles. Thank You for positioning us to possess more than we lost, and for sealing our territory with everlasting joy.

In Jesus' name, Amen.

DAY 24

Marvels Beyond Belief

"Behold, I work a work in your days, which you will not
believe though it be told you."
—Habakkuk 1:5 WEB

Sovereign Lord, the God of wonders, I lift up my voice to honor
You. You are the One who does marvelous works beyond human
comprehension. You are not limited by time, history, or the decrees
of men. I decree that my life and my family shall become the theater
of Your unbelievable wonders.

O God of enlargement, arise and scatter every enemy that has set
boundaries around my destiny. Every demonic verdict declaring
that I will not rise, I nullify you by fire. Every spiritual enemy that
whispers impossibility and defeat, I silence you with the Word of
the Living God. My territory expands by divine power, and my
inheritance cannot be stopped.

Lord, let the works You are doing in my life be so mighty that even
my enemies will marvel. Let sudden promotions, supernatural
breakthroughs, and generational blessings break forth from Your
throne. Let the captivity of years be overturned in one divine
moment of power.

Father, I thank You that You are working a work in my days—far
beyond imagination, beyond limitation, beyond what men have
ever seen. The enemy cannot stop it, the world cannot contain it,
and my life will never be the same. In Jesus' name, Amen.

DAY 25

SUMMONED TO EXPANSION

"I will signal for them and gather them; for I have redeemed them; and they will increase as they have increased. I will sow them among the peoples; and they will remember me in far countries; and they will live with their children, and will return."
—Zechariah 10:8–9 WEB

Lord of Hosts, the God who redeems and gathers, I bless Your holy name. You are the Caller of nations and the One who multiplies what is small. You signal, and creation responds. You summon, and destinies are aligned. Today, I decree that You are signaling enlargement over my life and my family.

Every power of scattering that has fought against our destiny, I rebuke you in the name of Jesus! No longer will my family be reduced, divided, or diminished. The voice of the Lord gathers us into abundance, restores our inheritance, and plants us securely in our allotted land.

Father, I declare increase over my children, multiplication over my household, and fruitfulness over the work of my hands. Wherever we have been forgotten or displaced, the trumpet of God is sounding our return. We are remembered, restored, and repositioned for global impact.

Thank You, Lord, for sowing me like a seed among the nations, that my influence will stretch beyond my borders. Thank You for making my lineage a banner of redemption, that generations may live and prosper under Your call.

In Jesus' name, Amen.

DAY 26

LIFE ABUNDANTLY FULL

"The thief only comes to steal, kill, and destroy. I came that
they may have life, and may have it abundantly."
—John 10:10 WEB

Lord Jesus, Giver of life, I worship You. You came not to give me
survival, but abundance. You came to destroy the works of the thief
and to release overflowing life into every part of my being. I stand
in that covenant promise today, declaring that death, destruction,
and barrenness have no authority over me and my household.

Every thief assigned to steal my inheritance, be destroyed by fire!
Every enemy designed to cut short my life and my family's joy, I
declare your works are cancelled by the power of Christ's blood. No
spirit of destruction will prevail over us; no plan of hell will devour
our portion.

I decree abundance over my family: abundant health, abundant
wisdom, abundant provision, abundant peace. My life shall be a
testimony of more than enough, my children shall rise into a
destiny overflowing with grace, and the works of our hands shall
multiply.

Lord, thank You for giving me life beyond limits—eternal, fruitful,
and overflowing. From this day, my family lives in abundance, and
no enemy can take it away.

In Jesus' name, Amen.

DAY 27

SHINING BRIGHTER DAILY

"But the path of the righteous is like the dawning light,
that shines more and more until the perfect day."
—Proverbs 4:18 WEB

Father of lights, I magnify You. You are the God who makes the righteous shine, and who turns small beginnings into blazing glory. I declare that my life and the life of my family shall shine brighter and brighter, never dimming, never retreating.

Every power that wants to keep us in darkness, I command you to be broken now. Every curse of stagnation and regression, I cancel by the blood of the Lamb. The enemy shall not dim our light, nor extinguish our destiny. We rise in brilliance, and our influence increases like the morning sun.

Lord, expand my path until no shadow of limitation remains. Let my light pierce through nations and generations. Cause my children to shine in righteousness and wisdom, becoming beacons of hope in a dark world.

I decree that my family is moving forward—never backward, never stuck, but shining, enlarging, and rising. The path of our destiny is unstoppable, and it glows until we stand perfected in Your presence.

In Jesus' name, Amen.

DAY 28

EXCEEDINGLY, ABUNDANTLY MORE

"Now to him who is able to do exceedingly abundantly above all that we ask or think, according to the power that works in us."
—Ephesians 3:20 WEB

Almighty God, El Shaddai, I honor You as the One who is more than enough. You are the God of exceeding abundance, the One who surpasses every imagination. I decree today that my life and my family will experience the overflow of Your mighty power.

Every limitation of the enemy that seeks to confine my vision, I shatter it now! Every wall of impossibility surrounding my household, be torn down by the exceeding greatness of His power. I declare that our prayers will be answered beyond request, our dreams fulfilled beyond imagination, and our destinies enlarged beyond calculation.

Father, release supernatural favor that carries us into places our strength could never reach. Let resources flow, doors open, and opportunities multiply until our lives testify of divine abundance. Let the power of Christ within me propel me into dimensions where only Your glory can explain the outcome.

I thank You, Lord, that no enemy can stop Your exceeding work in me. You are enlarging my family into greatness, and generations shall call us blessed.

In Jesus' name, Amen.

DAY 29

A Secure Dwelling

"'I will appoint a place for my people Israel, and will plant them, that they may dwell in their own place, and be moved no more. The children of wickedness will not afflict them any more, as at the first, and from the day that I commanded judges to be over my people Israel; and I will subdue all your enemies. Moreover I tell you that Yahweh will build you a house.'"
—1 Chronicles 17:9–10 WEB

Lord God, my Rock and my Dwelling Place, I praise You. You are the One who appoints a place and establishes Your people. You are the God who plants, secures, and builds. Today I stand on this covenant promise that my family and I shall dwell in safety, unshaken, and untouched by wickedness.

Every enemy assigned to uproot me from my inheritance, I command you to fall by the sword of the Lord! Every oppressor plotting to afflict my household, your time is over. The Lord has appointed my dwelling, and no power of darkness can remove me.

Father, plant me deeply in my territory. Make me immovable in my assignment, flourishing in the land You have given me. Subdue the enemies that rise against my children, and establish a generational house of glory and righteousness.

Thank You, Lord, for appointing a place where my family will prosper, increase, and never be afflicted again. Thank You for building us into a house of strength that no enemy can overthrow.

In Jesus' name, Amen.

DAY 30

SEEDS OF INCREASE

"Now may he who supplies seed to the sower and bread for food, supply and multiply your seed for sowing, and increase the fruits of your righteousness; you being enriched in everything for all generosity, which produces thanksgiving to God through us."
—2 Corinthians 9:10–11 WEB

Provider of every good gift, I bless Your name. You are the One who gives seed to the sower and multiplies every offering. You enrich Your children so that they may walk in generosity and overflow in righteousness. Today I decree that my life and my family are stepping into multiplication.

Every devourer assigned to eat my seed, I rebuke you in the name of Jesus! Every spirit of lack and poverty assigned against my household, I command you to be consumed by the fire of God. No longer will my seed be wasted or my harvest stolen.

Father, supply seed into my hands, and let every seed multiply into abundant harvest. Cause the fruits of righteousness in my family to flourish, that our influence may stretch to nations and our testimonies bring thanksgiving to Your name.

Thank You for enriching me in every way, that I may walk in generosity and overflow. Thank You for causing my family to live in such abundance that many will glorify Your name through our lives. In Jesus' name, Amen.

EPILOGUE

As you have journeyed through these thirty days of prophetic prayers, you have lifted the same cry that Jabez once prayed: *"Oh, that You would bless me indeed and enlarge my territory!"* This is not a cry of ambition, but of alignment—a call to step into the inheritance God already prepared for you before the foundations of the world. By faith, you have broken limitations, shattered barriers, and declared enlargement over your life and family.

Enlargement is not a one-time experience; it is a lifestyle of continual stretching. Every time you pray, believe, and act on God's Word, He pushes back the borders of confinement and opens new doors. Expansion is progressive—what you walked into today is only a foretaste of the greater spaces God is leading you into tomorrow. The enemy may attempt to resist, but remember: once God enlarges your borders, no power of darkness can confine you again.

As you move forward, keep declaring these prayers. Let them become the language of your spirit. Expect fresh territories in your walk with God, in your relationships, in your influence, and in your provision. Live with the conviction that God has called you beyond limits, destined you for fruitfulness, and appointed you to leave a legacy of enlargement that will echo through generations.

Go forth in faith. Step boldly into greater spaces. Walk in fruitfulness and overflow. And may your life forever testify of the God who hears, the God who enlarges, and the God who establishes. Your territory has already been marked by His hand. Now, arise and possess it.

In Jesus' name, Amen.

ENCOURAGE OTHERS WITH YOUR STORY

If this prayer guide has strengthened your faith, deepened your intercession, or helped you stand in the gap, would you consider leaving a short review on Amazon? Your feedback not only encourages others but also helps more believers discover this resource and join in the prayer movement. Every review—just a few sentences—makes a difference. Thank you for being part of this movement.

More from PrayerScripts

Command Your Destiny Series

Command Your Morning:

30 Days of Prayers and Declarations to Seize Your Day and Shape Your Destiny

There is a battle over every morning—and every believer must choose to either drift into the day or command it.

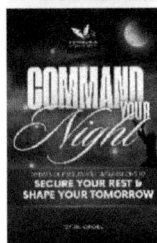

Command Your Night:

30 Days of Prayers and Declarations to Secure Your Rest and Shape Your Tomorrow

Every night is a spiritual battlefield—what you do before you sleep can determine the course of your tomorrow.

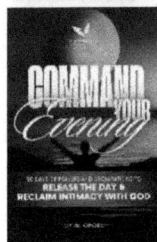

Command Your Evening:

30 Days of Prayers and Declarations to Release the Day and Reclaim Intimacy with God

There is a battle over every transition—and evening is one of the most spiritually neglected.

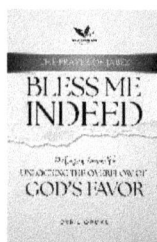

Bless Me Indeed:

Unlocking the Overflow of God's Favor

What if you could activate God's favor in your life today and walk in blessings that surpass your wildest expectations?

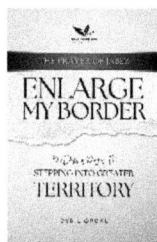

Enlarge My Border:

Stepping Into Greater Territory

Do you feel like you're living beneath your full potential? Do limitations, setbacks, and invisible barriers keep you from stepping into all God has promised? It's time to lift your cry for enlargement.

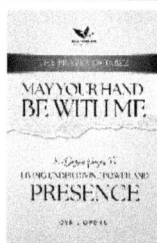

May Your Hand Be With Me:

Living Under Divine Power and Presence

What happens when the mighty hand of God rests upon your life? Doors open that no man can shut. Strength rises where weakness once prevailed. Guidance comes in the midst of confusion, and protection surrounds you in every battle.

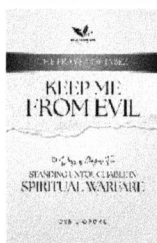

Keep Me From Evil:

Standing Untouchable in Spiritual Warfare

What if the enemy's plans could never touch you or your family? Imagine walking through life completely protected, untouchable, and victorious—no matter what schemes are formed against you.

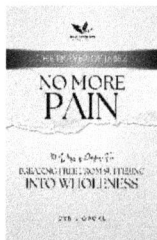

No More Pain:

Breaking Free from Suffering into Wholeness

Have you been carrying the weight of sorrow, disappointment, or hidden wounds for far too long? Do cycles of pain seem to repeat in your life, your marriage, or your family?

Discern the Enemy:

Sharpening Spiritual Perception to Recognize Satan's Tactics and Guard Your Destiny

The greatest danger is not the enemy you can see—it is the one you cannot. Can you recognize the enemy before he strikes?

Disarm the Enemy:

Stripping Satan of Weapons and Influence Through the Power of Christ

Are you tired of feeling like the enemy has the upper hand in your life? It's time to take back your ground, silence the lies of darkness, and walk in the unstoppable authority of Christ.

Destroy the Enemy:

Breaking Strongholds and Cancelling Evil Works by God's Authority

Are you tired of living under the weight of unseen battles? It's time to rise up and destroy the enemy's works in your life.

Deliver from the Enemy:

Calling on God's Power for Freedom, Rescue, and Lasting Victory

Break free from spiritual attacks and experience God's mighty deliverance in every battle.

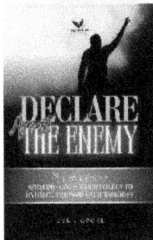

Declare Against the Enemy:

Speaking God's Word Boldly to Enforce Triumph Over Darkness

What if you could silence the enemy's schemes, protect your family, and walk boldly into every God-ordained assignment with unshakable authority?

Scriptures & Prayers for Deliverance from Trouble:

40 Days of Prayer for When Life Feels Overwhelming

Are you walking through a season where life feels heavy and your prayers feel weak?

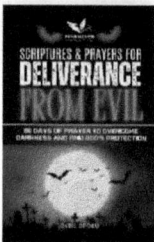

Scriptures & Prayers for Deliverance from Evil:

50 Days of Prayer to Overcome Darkness and Find God's Protection

When darkness presses in, how do you pray?

Scriptures & Prayers for Engaging the Enemy:

70 Days of Prayer to Rebuke the Enemy and Release God's Power

You weren't called to run from the battle—you were anointed to win it.

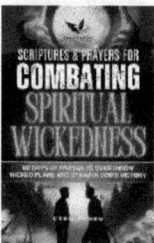

Scriptures & Prayers for Combating Spiritual Wickedness:

50 Days of Prayer to Overthrow Wicked Plans and Stand in God's Victory

Are you facing opposition that feels deeper than the natural? You're not imagining it—and you're not powerless.

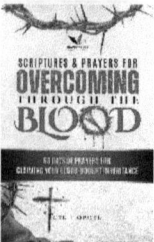

Scriptures & Prayers for Overcoming Through the Blood:

60 Days of Prayers for Claiming Your Blood-Bought Inheritance

You were never meant to fight sin, fear, or Satan in your own strength.

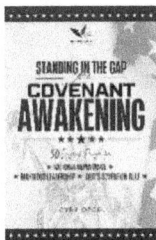

Standing in the Gap for Covenant Awakening:

30 Days of Prayer for National Repentance, Righteous Leadership & God's Sovereign Rule

What if your prayers could help turn the tide of a nation?

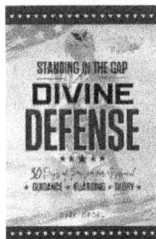

Standing in the Gap for Divine Defense:

30 Days of Prayer for National Guidance, Guarding & Glory

When the foundations of a nation feel as if they're shaking, prayer is the strongest fortress you can build.

Standing in the Gap for National Healing:

40 Days of Prayer for Reconciliation, Righteousness, and Restoration

What if your prayers could help heal a nation? What if God is waiting for someone—like you—to stand in the gap?

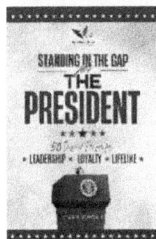

Standing in the Gap for The President:

50 Days of Prayer for Leadership, Loyalty, and Lifeline

When a nation's leader is under spiritual siege, will you answer the call to stand in the gap?

Pardon Through the Blood:

60 Days of Prayers for Total Forgiveness and Freedom

Guilt is a prison. The blood of Jesus holds the key.

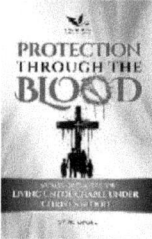

Protection Through the Blood:

60 Days of Prayers for Living Untouchable Under Christ's Blood

You are not helpless. You are not exposed. You are covered—completely—by the blood of Jesus.

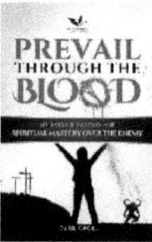

Prevail Through the Blood:

60 Days of Prayers for Spiritual Mastery Over the Enemy

What if every scheme of the enemy against your life could be dismantled—by one unstoppable weapon?

Preservation Through the Blood:

60 Days of Prayers for Divine Healing and Wholeness

Unlock Lasting Healing and Wholeness Through the Blood of Jesus

Prosperity Through the Blood:

60 Days of Prayers for Unlocking Heaven's Wealth and Walking in Covenant Increase

You were redeemed for more than survival—you were redeemed to prosper.

Peace Through the Blood:

60 Days of Prayers for Resting in the Covenant of Unshakable Peace

Are you ready to silence every storm of the mind, heart, and home—once and for all?

www.ingramcontent.com/pod-product-compliance
Lightning Source LLC
Chambersburg PA
CBHW062026040426
42447CB00010B/2154